Individual
Coconut Cake
$5.

New York
Cheesecake
$5.

W9-CZJ-403

cake expressions

Cake
expressions

by dottie smith

*To Jenny —
Enjoy.
Dottie*

A publication of Hoffman Media, LLC

Birmingham, Alabama

copyright

First published in 2006 by Hoffman Media, LLC
Birmingham, Alabama

With offices at:
1900 International Park Drive, Suite 50
Birmingham, Alabama 35243
www.hoffmanmedia.com

ISBN 0-9785489-3-0
Printed in the United States of America

Publishers of *Southern Lady* magazine

dedication

May this compilation of words and ideas honor our

Father in heaven, my Lord and my Savior, Jesus Christ, who has given

me hope in a life with none, and peace that surpasses all understanding.

Without Him everything is a futile attempt at happiness.

To Terry, the love of my life, my best friend, and

my inspiration. If not for you, I would never have

believed I could accomplish so much.

acknowledgements

Although this book has one author's name, it is truly the work of a team of talented individuals. I want to thank each person who worked to help my dream of a book about cakes become a reality.

Antonia and her staff are my hands. Whatever I dream, their hands can make. My desire is for you to know the happiness God wants for you. Your talent is a gift from Him.

My sincere thanks and appreciation goes to **our employee family**. This book would not be possible without your dedication and drive to be the best.

My stepsons, **Tyler and Austin**, who love me despite my faults and mistakes, have fully supported me as I have worked on this book. They have understood when my time was short and when my attention was on cakes. I love you.

My mom and dad, **Mary Ruth and Sam Freeman,** and my sisters, **Linda, Nancy, Jan, and Darri**, have loved me unconditionally and have always supported Terry and me. Thank you.

Terry's parents, **Kelley Edgar**—the namesake of our company—and **Lillie Ruth Smith,** have worked with us at the bakery. Your support means so much.

Phyllis Hoffman, president of Hoffman Media, thank you for your encouragement. You are a gifted woman of God, and an artisan in every sense of the word. **Brian Hoffman,** you are my biggest cheerleader; you started it all.

I am so grateful to all of **my friends** who supported me through this wild and wonderful journey. I could not have made it without you.

Working with the Hoffman Media staff to bring this book to life has been a wonderful experience. **Yukie McLean,** style director, used her incredible sense of style and beauty to present each cake in an artistic manner. **Jodi Daniels,** art director, used color to convey a theme that is inspirational and has crafted a work of art with each page. **Clare Martin,** assistant editor, has taken my thoughts and scribbled notes and turned them into a work of eloquence. **Mac Jamieson,** creative director, made the cake settings come alive with his artful eye. **Marcy Black and Arden Ward,** photographers, saw beauty through the small lens of the camera. Thank you for teaching me so much. **Stacey Norwood,** writer, and **Karen Dauphin,** editorial assistant, worked tirelessly to ensure the project would be perfect for the readers. **Delisa McDaniel,** color technician, worked to ensure the colors would be flawless. **Greg Baugh,** production director, kept us focused on meeting our goals. **Barbara Cockerham,** editor, orchestrated the efforts of the team and helped us create a beautiful book. My wish, as you read this book, is that it will bring you pleasure and joy.

table of contents

introduction

"I'll bake a cake."

So often these words are spoken as a celebration draws near. The occasion always calls for cake—whether a homey holiday, a milestone event, a grand affair, or simply a moment when we need a little slice of comfort.

I remember vividly the cakes my mother made as I was growing up. The warm, buttery aroma would curl out of the oven and waft through the whole house. And then there was the frosting—mounds of butter creamed together with sugar, a combination that eventually provided the inspiration for the buttercream frosting we make at Edgar's Old Style Bakery. As a child, I never understood why the cake had to cool before it could be frosted—that was a lesson that would be learned later. What I did know then was the sound of my mother's mixer whirring in the kitchen meant there would certainly be a battle between my four sisters and me to determine who got the most frosting-laden beater to lick clean.

On birthdays, it wasn't the sound of the mixer that drew us to the kitchen, but rather the presence of a white box from a local bakery. Peeking inside, we were inevitably greeted with a snowy white cake adorned with tiny, sparkling

toys—an enchanted fairyland imagined in sugar. To this day, the sweetly acrid smell of wisps of smoke mixed with melted candle wax after a round of "Happy Birthday" has been sung still makes me feel that same tickle of wonder and awe I felt as a child, come birthday time.

It is my wish that everyone should have such lasting memories, and I am honored to be able to play a part in their creation. Owning a bakery is far from a glamorous profession— every gorgeous cake we produce entails hours spent in front of the oven, mixer, or finishing table. But it is a profession that imparts a deep sense of fulfillment. To know that you are a part, however large or small, of the most precious moments of a person's life is extremely gratifying. It is this knowledge that gives me the drive to always do better, to always exceed expectations.

Edgar's Old Style Bakery opened its doors in 1998 and began producing specialty cakes, pastries, breads, and other baked goods. The bakery has since expanded, increasing to three locations in the Birmingham, Alabama metro area, and now also offers a continental breakfast and lunch menu. Along with a steady and growing customer base, Edgar's also received Alabama's Silver Award for Retailer of the Year.

Over the years, I have had the opportunity to work with many customers on the daunting task of choosing the perfect cake to complement an event—be it a birthday, wedding, baby shower, or graduation. These days, we don't always have time to do the baking ourselves when planning a celebration, yet we still want to be involved in the details of the cake's design and taste.

Drawing on my years of experience, I have written this book with the hope that it will serve as a guide, helping you make informed and, yes, creative choices when planning your own special occasions. And although I have included a few of our favorite recipes, this book is not intended to be a tutorial on how to replicate these fabulous cakes. Rather, I hope it will inspire you to create your own works of art, using your imagination and skill.

Whether you are planning a wedding for 500 guests or an intimate gathering for two, wherever there is a celebration, there should also be cake.

special occasions

Serene Setting

WHEN SUMMER FIRST ARRIVES, IT seems as if the long, lazy days will last forever—but in reality, they tend to evaporate like the grassy dew of a June morning. With children home from school and family vacations looming on the horizon, sometimes it's nice to take a few moments to simply stop and savor the coming season before we're buried in a flurry of fun.

Last summer, I decided to have a few of my girlfriends over for a last-minute luncheon to offer us all the chance to relax and visit with one another before our lives became too hectic to do so. I settled on a color scheme of blue and white, reminiscent of calm, cool waters, which I punctuated with bits of yellow in a nod to summer's abundant sunshine.

Individual two-tiered angel food cakes, topped with a light, airy buttercream frosting and perky yellow daisies were a perfect way to make each guest feel honored— and tempt them to linger just a little longer.

I used the cobalt blue color of the stemware and the delicate etched lines of the blue and white transferware as inspiration for the decoration of the petite cakes. Tiny yellow daisies made of rolled fondant provide a nice contrast to the swirling lines of vibrant blue. Miniature crystal cake stands show off the individual desserts in a way that is formal enough to be feminine, yet casual enough for an outdoor get-together.

beautiful

Creating a beautiful environment for your guests doesn't have to involve weeks—or even days—of advance planning. For this gathering, I simply pulled an eclectic mix of tableware from the china cabinet and accented it with peonies snipped from a friend's garden. A bit of wispy yellow polka-dotted fabric from my closet tied to the backs of the chairs completed the inviting, summery look.

Run for the Roses

I HAVE ALWAYS HAD A PARTICULAR FONDNESS FOR HORSES. From my earliest days on my family's farm, I can remember watching in awe as my sisters galloped by on Buddy, a bay quarter horse, and Missy, a dark bay mare. Although at a young age I found the horses a bit intimidating, I loved feeding them sugar cubes, always minding my mother's instructions to keep my hand flat so the hungry animals wouldn't nip my fingers.

Perhaps it is these memories that generate such a fever every year for the first weekend in May. In the days leading up to the Kentucky Derby, I pore over the statistics of each horse and jockey to determine which will receive my cheers.

Whether I'm watching the race live at Churchill Downs or from the comfort of my own living room, I always place a call to my mother afterwards to ponder the outcome and make fervent wishes that the winner will go on to take the Triple Crown. Such excitement is certainly a call for a celebration, and so, in a garden overflowing with the Derby's signature red flower, I paid tribute to all the glamour and splendor of the Run for the Roses.

hats

In the spirit of the Kentucky Derby's unofficial dress code, I always request that each guest come to the party wearing a favorite hat. During the celebration, everyone is asked to share the story behind their chapeaux before all the hats are grouped together on a table to create a festive display.

traditions

Two cakes, each of which represents a particular piece of Derby tradition, crown the serving table. Made of devil's food cake with buttercream and fondant frosting, this delicate wide-brimmed blue hat is similar to the elaborate toppers donned by the ladies at Churchill Downs. The second cake, a butter yellow round separated by layers of strawberry cream cheese filling, is topped with the same roses that customarily encircle the Derby winner's neck.

How did we make the hat brim? See Page 138

The winner's garland at Churchill Downs is made of more than 550 red roses, with a "crown" in the center—a single scarlet bloom pointing skyward to symbolize the drive and spirit that is necessary to take home the winner's title. Because that symbol is so central to the Kentucky Derby, I always try to outfit my own party with as many red roses as possible. In addition to the rosebushes that meander through the garden, I scattered a parade of lovely containers brimming with flowers, and at each place setting, I presented the famed roses with another item made famous by the Derby—a sterling silver mint julep cup.

At the Kentucky Derby, only one competitor walks away a winner—but at my party, I like to make sure every person who attends receives such VIP treatment. As they leave, each guest is presented with a petite, rose-embellished confection created from light layers of white cake and covered in poured sugar frosting.

Adventures in Cake

I CAN'T SAY *ALICE'S ADVENTURES IN WONDERLAND* IS MY UNQUESTIONED favorite book from childhood, but the colorful jumble of characters and occasions in the Lewis Carroll classic certainly made an impression. My favorite character in the book by far is the March Hare, who leads Alice down the rabbit hole, and who later joins her for tea with the Mad Hatter and the dormouse. The memorable images of that long-ago story inspired me to create a tea party for my grown-up girlfriends. The topsy-turvy cake I created, reminiscent of the Mad Hatter's unique top hat, is made even more colorful by the swirls, whirls, and free-form designs found also in the teawares.

artful

I found this artful tea service at a favorite boutique during an afternoon shopping excursion. The brilliant colors are fresh and feminine, while the tea set's bold design made the service a perfect pick for the theme. Even the time-conscious March Hare would stop for a moment to drink in this beautiful tablescape.

How do you order from a bakery? See Page 142

whimsical

I replicated the hearts from the teapot by piping on buttercream and sprinkling the hearts with pearl dust. I also created whimsical pointed flowers of fondant to mirror the other patterns found in the china. The yellow rolled fondant flowers add a floral touch that isn't constrained by too much tradition.

Farm Fresh

SOME OF MY MOST VIVID AND HAPPIEST CHILDHOOD MEMORIES are of time spent on my family's farm. Although a day at the farm almost always meant hard work—whether it was tending to the bountiful vegetable garden or taking care of our stable of horses—it also meant a chance to enjoy the charms that only wide-open country spaces can offer.

For a summertime party, held before the heat of the day has descended, I wanted to give other children a chance to see, touch, and taste the joys of life on the farm.

My neighbors, the Gilberts—who have built their home in the midst of 80 magnificent acres of fresh meadows and wooded forest—provided the perfect setting for such a celebration on a dewy summer morning. The Gilberts' twelve grandchildren proved an especially receptive audience for a sugary mid-morning selection of sweets: fanciful ladybug and dragonfly cookies; cupcakes adorned with buttercream cows, pigs, and chicks; and the feather in our cap—a mama hen cake to watch over the whole brood.

Rather than mold miniature farm characters from marzipan, I opted to figure-pipe the cupcake toppers from buttercream frosting. Using a variety of colors and tips, I created plump, jovial pigs, cows, ducks, and chickens. Because children generally adore the taste of buttercream, I used other types of icing sparingly—rolled fondant only makes an appearance on the barnyard-scene cake in the form of the field, the pond, and the daffodil leaves. Royal icing is used to create the white picket fence, which, by design, mirrors the one that surrounds the Gilberts' antebellum-style home.

Cookie cutters come in practically any shape, size, and motif you can imagine. At the bakery, we live by the motto "the bigger, the better" when it comes to choosing cutters for our cookie treats. For our down-on-the-farm festivities, I created giant butterflies, frogs, dragonflies, and ladybugs for the children to enjoy as they played. A few leftover cookies were fitted with lollipop sticks and wrapped in cellophane to be taken home as a souvenir from the morning at Grandma's.

The hen cake is always a popular request at the bakery during the spring and early summer months. In my experience, many people associate the image of a mother hen perched protectively over her nest of soon-to-be chicks with the nurturing seasons of renewal. A basket-weave tip helps form the nest from brown buttercream, while creamy white frosting piped through a leaf tip creates wonderfully fluffy faux feathers.

daisy

Part of what makes a farm setting so appealing is the abundance of flowers that grow in colorful patches, confined by neither hand nor element. I chose one of these wildflowers, the daisy, to adorn a sunny yellow layer cake that served as a companion to the mama hen. And of course, the cheerful blossoms—affixed with a dab of lemony buttercream filling—wouldn't be complete without a few gum-paste butterflies flitting about for company.

relax

Resting in the shadow of the barn, a diminutive playhouse, complete with curtains, window boxes, and a front porch, is a cherished play spot for the Gilberts' grandchildren. Picnic tables whimsically decorated with playful polka-dot china, bandanna-style linens, and cherry tomato plants provided an informal, summery setting for the children to enjoy their cake, while the adults in the bunch could relax and savor the outdoors from the rustic comfort of white Adirondack chairs.

Pumpkin Patch

LATE AUGUST USUALLY FINDS ME OUTSIDE AMONG MY FLOWERS, trying in vain to revive weathered geraniums and drooping dahlias. My sadness at seeing the last of summer's bounty trickle away, however, is softened by the onset of autumn. As is the case every year, the moment inevitably arrives when I feel the caress of a cool, crisp breeze across my face—a sure sign that fall is on the horizon. That moment brings with it the knowledge that within the span of a few weeks, we will bid goodbye to the long, carefree days of summer and witness the dawn of a new season—one of bountiful pumpkins and chrysanthemums, of glorious, colorful sugar maples, of football and fuzzy sweaters.

I view fall not as a season to pine for the summery days of lazy cookouts and pool parties, but rather a chance to savor a new sensation. Clear skies, crisp air, and brilliant colors give us leave to relish the excitement of family holidays to come. In this spirit, I designed a cake-filled celebration to capture all that is beautiful about autumn. The warm rich hues that saturate the season are represented both in the décor and in the flowers of the centerpiece cake. And as a special treat, I included a sugary homage to fall's most everlasting symbol: the pumpkin.

How did we create the flowers? See Page 136

Arranged in a hand-hewn rectangular dough bowl, miniature pumpkin cakes make a darling centerpiece. Topped with sugar-paste stems and leaves, these lilliputian confections are as delicious as they are lovely. In keeping with the season, the other elements that comprise the tablescape are equally rustic, from homespun wicker chargers and sturdy crockeryware to a touch of autumn elegance at each place setting. A single, perfect leaf placed on each individual plate not only adds a hint of color, but a note of whimsy as well.

pumpkins

The crop of cakes for our fall festival was inspired by the pretty pumpkins that grow in the patch that thrives each fall on our family farm. From pumpkinesque dollops of buttercream atop single-serving cupcakes to a selection of pumpkin-shaped cakes, I wanted to maximize the use of my favorite autumn symbol. To create the pumpkin cakes, we baked two devil's food cakes in standard-size Bundt pans, then inverted one on top of the other to give the cake its rotund shape. As we iced the cakes, we carved away pieces here and there, rendering a final product that was not perfectly round, in an inadvertent mimicry of nature's own beautifully inexact design.

Hat Trick
Sweet Surprise
Bridal Charm
April Showers
Something Blue
Baby Mine

milestones

Hat Trick

AS A CHILD, I LOVED ATTENDING BIRTHDAY PARTIES, where, inevitably, each guest would be presented with a festive party hat. Those cardboard toppers were our little-girl versions of the gorgeous chapeaux our mothers wore for only the most special of occasions. Of course, today's party hats are much more elaborate than the cardboard affairs of my girlhood. At the bakery, we stock beautiful, brightly colored cloth hats festooned with flowers, ribbons, and tulle. These over-the-top accessories were my inspiration for creating imaginative cakes for an extra-special birthday party. Three larger cakes are displayed in the center of the table, and each guest was presented with a smaller, but no less intricately detailed, individual cake—ensuring the tradition of presenting every party guest with a little something special is passed down to a new generation.

cakes

Their cone shapes require these cakes be extremely dense. Devil's food—or pound cake, if chocolate is not preferred—will support the rolled fondant molded around each cake. The ribbons and other fanciful decorations are made from hand-rolled fondant.

How did we create ribbons? See Page 135

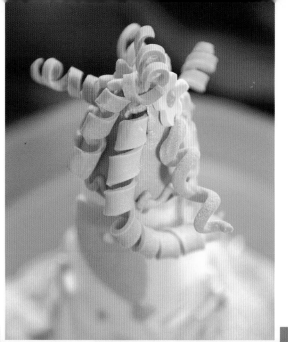

shimmer

The hint of shimmer on the cakes' surface comes from a wonderful product called pearl dust. The tiny vials of glittery, pixie-dust-like powder, available in a range of colors, are a vital part of any baker's cache of tools. I love to brush a bit of pearl dust over fondant icing when the occasion calls for a little extra sparkle.

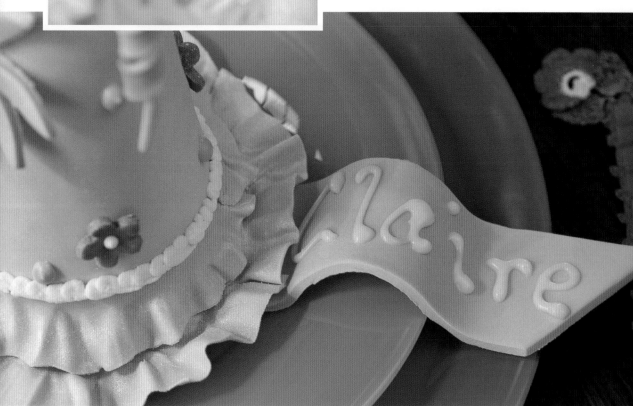

special

To make the individual cakes even more special, I tucked a wide ribbon of fondant underneath each one and printed the child's name on it. These personalized streamers can accompany each cake in lieu of place cards, or you may choose to spotlight only the birthday girl's cake in this manner.

Like the cakes, several of the other decorative elements used throughout the party take cues from the celebration itself. Brightly wrapped birthday presents piled on a side table form an eye-catching display, while the party hats that served as the inspiration for the birthday cakes are suspended above their frosted counterparts. Plenty of white tulle, brightly colored ribbons, and cheerful Gerber daisies fill in extra spaces and help tie the whole theme together.

When decorating for a child's party, both color and scale are paramount. For the color scheme of this party, I echoed the vivid, saturated hues of the hats, as these are appropriate for a wide range of ages. When designing the table setting, I made sure every element was considered from a child's perspective. Jewel-toned, old-fashioned sundae glasses are the perfect size for smaller hands to hold, while brightly colored plates add an element of style, and are durable enough for children to use without worry.

Sweet Surprise

FOR ME, THE ACT OF GIVING A GIFT IS INFINITELY MORE EXCITING than receiving one. The expression of joy that crosses the recipient's face upon opening a perfectly wrapped present is a gift unto itself. When birthday celebrations are in order, such pretty packages sometimes take the form of a cake, allowing the party's hostess to express her well wishes to the guest of honor through a treat all can enjoy.

It was with this in mind that I created one of the bakery's most popular designs, which we lovingly refer to as "the bow cake." Fashioned to resemble beautifully wrapped packages bound by oversized bows, these cakes can accommodate almost anyone's personal taste and style. For a springtime birthday celebration, I chose to display an array of pastel-colored cakes, each bearing its own unique color scheme. I spotlighted the colorful cakes—in a rainbow of bubblegum shades—by keeping the rest of the décor minimal. An antique white tablecloth and crystal cake pedestals let the pinks, purples, yellows, and greens steal the show.

Creating a gorgeous tablescape doesn't have to entail hard work—it merely requires a little attention to detail. To create a conversation-starting centerpiece, I placed a slightly larger cake on a raised pedestal, then surrounded it with smaller versions, which were placed at an angle to draw the eye. Taking a cue from the cakes' pastel tones, I sparingly pulled in similar hues against the white backdrop of the tablecloth. Chargers tinted in sherbet shades sit under each dessert plate, while napkins in contrasting colors grace the parfait glasses at each setting.

How did we make the bows? See Page 133

Bridal Charm

OVER THE YEARS, I HAVE NOTICED A TREND DEVELOPING AMONG young brides and grooms. More and more, many young couples are choosing to forego the traditional walk down the aisle in front of family and friends in favor of smaller ceremonies in more exotic locales.

Saying "I do" under the balmy shade of palm trees or in a quaint villa perched on a snow-capped mountain may be every bit as romantic as a traditional ceremony, but destination weddings do pose a singular dilemma: how to include friends and loved ones in the big day. I recently helped a dear friend solve that very quandary. Her son, who was planning to wed in St. John, wanted to bring together loved ones to celebrate this joyous occasion, but not everyone could attend the island ceremony. As a solution, I hosted a bridal tea and reception, giving the couple's loved ones the chance to honor their union a bit closer to home.

As the men headed to the golf course happily outfitted with homemade BLT sandwiches and jars of iced tea, the women stayed behind for a girls-only celebration of matrimony. Together, we sipped tea, nibbled finger sandwiches, and enjoyed the petit fours. Later in the afternoon, the two parties came together to toast the happy couple and look on as they cut the first piece of their unique, hydrangea-topped wedding cake.

Because no wedding celebration is complete without the inclusion of "something old," I chose several pieces of heirloom crystal belonging to the mother of the groom—including her crystal vases and candlesticks—and supplemented those with some from my own collection. And while the antique-looking wedding cake topper had a distinctly timeless feel, it's actually brand new—we carry the retro-inspired adornments at the bakery. The inspired combination of old and new is not only beautiful, sentimental, and perfect for the occasion, it is also reminiscent of all that is lovely about springtime.

To reflect a fresh beginning for the couple, as well as the dawning of a new season, I wanted the celebration of their nuptials to evoke the budding life of spring. Pansies are perched on petit fours, sunny yellow jonquils and sunflowers dance down the tiers of one cake, and the other showcases regal white lilies with brilliant green leaves. The lush, verdant color, one that symbolizes newness and rebirth, was a primary element for the overall color scheme, from the celadon tablecloths, to the glossy green leaves of the tulips arranged in bunches, to the gum-paste hydrangeas that adorn the two-tiered wedding cake.

Join
from four until six o'cl...
for champagne and dessert
to celebrate
the coming marriage
of
Allison & Karl
2010 Legacy Drive
Greystone

You are cordially invited to a
Bridal Tea
honoring
Allison Rowland
Sunday, February 26th
two until four o'clock
2010 Legacy Drive
Greystone
*Teresa Earnest   Donna Weitman

An invitation is the first glimpse your guests will have of your wedding celebration. It is my belief that the look and feel of the invitation helps establish the tone of the party. For this bridal tea, I mirrored the celadon green used in the party decorations in a die-cut pattern of clustered, springlike white flowers. I never mind indulging a little on a pretty invitation. In my mind, it's well worth the splurge.

April Showers

MANY TIMES IT SEEMS THAT CAKES PLAY SECOND FIDDLE to other party embellishments—fanciful centerpieces, elaborate table settings, and bountiful fresh flowers.

For a bridal shower staged in late spring, I wanted to rethink the traditional formula and let the cakes themselves serve as the serving table's sole decoration. To this end, I crafted a three-tiered cake, featuring a variety of spring and summer blossoms cascading from layer to layer. I surrounded the springtime showstopper with a selection of smaller rounds, each of which draws on elements presented in the centerpiece cake.

The only enhancement needed for this fanciful display was an assortment of crystal cake pedestals in varying heights, drawn from my collection at the bakery and bolstered with a couple of heirloom Fostoria pieces belonging to the hostess's mother, as well as my own mother. The hostess also allowed us to borrow from her collection of antique linens, which were placed under the cake pedestals to further highlight the ladylike whimsy of the arrangement.

flavors

A cluster of cakes in miniature presents a charming solution to serving a large group. Not only does the arrangement bring a dash of the unexpected to the table, but it also allows guests to choose from a variety of different flavors, taking a bit of each or a serving of one. The cakes for this bridal tea included strawberry filled with cream cheese frosting, devil's food with a mocha filling, and a yellow cake with strawberry cream cheese filling.

décor

For these decorative beauties, I drew inspiration not only from Mother Nature, but also from the décor of the room in which the party was being held. The room's buttery yellow walls provide a perfect canvas for the cakes, which are bursting with the colors of spring. I love the contrast of sunny yellow jonquils alongside lilac-hued violets and vibrant red roses. The quiet riot of colors is not unlike a spring garden in full bloom.

When creating flowers like these daffodils, hydrangeas, lilies of the valley, sunflowers, and roses, I never try to replicate exactly what is found in nature. I would certainly fall short trying to re-create God's handiwork, so instead I like to take a few artistic liberties with color and scale, resulting in a spray of truly unique blooms.

How did we create the flowers? See Page 136

To create a cake as elaborate as the one that served as the centerpiece for this bridal shower, more than few hours must be devoted to the process. The sugar-based flowers are created separately, a few days before the cake is made, then attached once it has been frosted. The effect is similar to adding jewelry to a beautiful outfit just before dashing out the door.

Something Blue

THE TOKENS FOR LUCK ON A BRIDE'S BIG DAY ARE FAMILIAR TO MOST of us: something old, something new, something borrowed, and something blue. These must-have good luck charms are outlined in a singsong rhyme that is believed to have originated during the Victorian era. However, the color blue has been used in weddings for centuries. In ancient Rome, brides wore blue to connote love, modesty, and fidelity, and the color's symbolic meaning has carried through to the present.

These days, brides are becoming more and more creative when finding "something blue" for their wedding day, whether it's an antique cameo worn at the neck or baby blue satin heels tucked under a flowing tulle skirt. For a country club wedding at which the primary color was a rich chocolate brown, I seized the opportunity to present the couple with a unique take on "something blue." The vibrant turquoise fondant that covers their elegant four-tiered wedding cake provides a stunning contrast with weightier chocolate stripes and roses.

sophistication

This wedding had a very tailored aesthetic, and I felt stripes would be the ideal way to express this polished sophistication on the cake, as well as mirror the striped pattern the bride chose for her reception décor. To give the eyes a rest between tiers, I chose to use stripes on every other cake layer. In an effort to bring an element of softness without sacrificing any of the cake's simple elegance, I added chocolate fondant roses.

The groom's affinity for golf made the country club's trophy room, which honors past club champions, the perfect location to display an elegant chocolate-on-chocolate groom's cake. Reminiscing about golfing legends past proved an enjoyable diversion for the men as they toasted the new groom.

The art of the wedding toast is as drenched in tradition and decorum as any other facet of the happy day. Etiquette dictates the best man is the first to raise his glass and toast the happy couple. He is typically followed by the groom, who toasts his new bride and her family, and afterwards, the fathers of both of the newlyweds raise a glass to their children's happiness. Finally, the bride and groom, champagne glasses in hand, ceremonially salute each other.

crystal

Though it is a time-honored tradition to bestow gifts of fine crystal upon couples celebrating the fifteenth year of their union, today's bride may wish to begin building her collection much sooner. The crystal candlesticks used at the reception were part of the bride's trousseau of beautiful wedding gifts, and made a simple and sophisticated grouping that was in keeping with the rest of the décor.

Baby Mine

A BABY SHOWER NOT ONLY OFFERS A MOTHER-TO-BE THE chance to share her joy, but also affords the opportunity for those same loved ones to bestow upon her many of the essential items she will need once her bundle of joy arrives. Though a baby-bootie-topped sheet cake in a gender-appropriate color is certainly an option, it seems a rather generic expression for such a blessed event. The message need not always be spelled out so blatantly for guests—it's certainly possible to adhere to traditional baby-shower sensibilities while livening things up with a twist or two.

For an expectant friend who happened to be very fond of polka dots, choosing a design scheme was simple, especially since her soon-to-be-born baby was a girl. I let those two parameters dictate every element of the gathering, from the dotted cupcakes and petit fours to the bold glassware. And the centerpiece, a cotton-candy pink tiered cake outfitted with retro dots, proves that an old-fashioned occasion doesn't have to translate into antiquated notions about style.

pink

The key to using only one color when decorating is to vary the shades so your guests' senses aren't overwhelmed. Pink proved to be a wonderful choice for a monochromatic theme, as it offers a wide range of hues from which to choose. Baby pink, bubblegum, magenta, and mauve—all reside in colorful harmony with one another. Sparing hints of white also helped to subtly punctuate the party's pretty-in-pink tablescape.

While I tried to shy away from as many stereotypical baby shower accoutrements as I could, I just couldn't resist a few nods to tradition. A friend's doll-sized wicker baby buggy proved the perfect place to stash linens and cups next to the punchbowl.

silver

Once more, I paid homage to tradition, while maintaining a forward style for my friend's shower. Sterling silver baby cups are customary at most showers, so I filled clusters of cups with baby's breath for decorative flair. These precious keepsakes can also be engraved for a personalized, elegant touch.

stork Meet the bakery's newest addition, Sebastian the Stork. For our pink-infused fête, our long-legged friend delivered a very different kind of bundle of joy than one might expect. Sebastian was kind enough to cradle a basket filled with cupcakes for hungry guests to nibble on throughout the party.

Sentimental Sweets
Easter Elegance
Mother's Heirlooms
Stars & Stripes
Night Before Christmas

holidays

Sentimental Sweets

SENTIMENTAL IS A WORD WITH MANY NUANCES. For some people, the word evokes maudlin expressions of emotion, but to me, sentimental conjures images of those things from the past that we cherish and protect. In the busy world we live in today, one of the things we seem to have sacrificed is simply connecting, on a daily basis, with the people we love.

That is why, to me, Valentine's Day is such an important holiday, and an intimate lunch for two is the perfect way to have uninterrupted time with your sweetheart or another loved one. For just such an occasion, I decided to create small individual cakes, each with a rose on top that represents love. The use of soft pink, lilac, cream, and ivory adds an extra touch of sweetness to the unabashedly sentimental sensibility of the occasion.

surprise

These petite cakes look so much like the kind of old-fashioned porcelain jewelry or keepsake boxes you might find on your mother's vanity. I can remember as a little girl sneaking into my own mother's room, lifting the lids on those trinket holders and longing to wear the beauties tucked away inside. Perhaps it is that memory that spurred these little lovelies, which, like jewelry boxes, hold a sweet surprise inside. Each cake is made with a different flavored filling—cherry walnut, chocolate espresso, and strawberry cream.

Easter & Elegance

EASTER IS A HOLIDAY THAT, THROUGH BOTH MEANING and occasion, symbolizes renewal of life—and nowhere is that more evident than in the South, where dogwoods and azaleas seem to bloom just for the occasion. This ethereal aesthetic is also evident in the pastel parade of beautiful new bonnets streaming through houses of worship on that special Sunday morning. Even the secular symbols of Easter—baby bunnies and fuzzy yellow chicks—remind us of the sweetness and innocence of a life just beginning.

To pay tribute to this singularly special occasion, I wanted to weave all these colorful elements together for an Easter celebration that makes use of the gorgeous shades of the season. Festive pinks, greens, blues, and yellows set the backdrop for a white-on-white dogwood blossom confection made of light, springy angel food cake with a sweet cherry filling. Deceptively simple, the cake reminds us of the pristine sentiment we honor on this holy day.

sprinkles

Cupcakes always make a charming addition to an array of larger layer cakes. For this party, I chose to let cupcakes serve as both a sort of dessert appetizer as well part of the overall décor. A basket placed in the foyer filled with cupcakes topped with pastel buttercream and a rainbow of confetti sprinkles immediately sets the color scheme for the event—and gives guests a little something to nibble on before lunch is served.

For family affairs such as this one, I always try to have a variety of cakes present that will appeal to all ages. While the centerpiece dogwood cake strikes a more refined tone, baby blue layer cakes decorated with soft green grass, chubby bunnies, and downy chicks are pure fun for pint-sized guests. I couldn't resist including our "Funny Bunny" sheet cake—one of my own personal favorites, as well as a perennial favorite of young ones.

Mother's Heirlooms

OF ALL THE GIFTS PASSED ON TO US BY OUR MOTHERS, BOTH LITERAL AND FIGURATIVE, I count heirloom china among the most valuable of those hand-me-down treasures. A table set with mother's heirlooms is a place where memories come to life over and over. My dear friend Ellen is in possession of such a set of dinnerware, which originally belonged to her great-grandmother—and I was thrilled to have it as both the backdrop and the inspiration for a Mother's Day luncheon staged in Ellen's home. The dainty, intricate patterns that dance across the china's surface are mirrored in the cakes that compose the pastel spread. On a day that honors our mothers, I can think of no better tribute than to have a selection of her special heirlooms, handed down from generation to generation, as the focus of the celebration.

Ellen's heirloom china dictated not only the colors and patterns I chose for the cakes but also for the other decorative items that graced the table. The linens drew inspiration from the pinks and blues found in the flowers on the heirloom tableware. In turn, the dancing porcelain ladies adorned in those same colors draw the eye to a silver basket of spring flowers in the same soft hues.

The soft pastel buttercream flowers that decorate each cake also, by design, lend the feeling of dining in a serene garden. For this occasion, I chose to have life imitate art, as the case may be, flinging open the French doors leading to Ellen's rose garden just outside. This allowed guests to see this lovely oasis and dine by the delicate music of water trickling from the fountain in the background.

How do we slice a round cake? See Page 141

In generations past, when the art of dining was typically observed with more formality than is often the case today, a beautiful table would be laden with the many unique dishes needed to serve a multitude of courses. For me, one of the creative challenges about heirloom pieces is coming up with new uses for these vintage treasures. For our Mother's Day luncheon, I discovered a delightful solution, nestling flower-topped petit fours in tiny antique compotes.

Stars & Stripes

NO INDEPENDENCE DAY CELEBRATION WOULD BE COMPLETE without a stunning volley of fireworks to end the evening— you could even say the sparkling display takes the cake. With this in mind, I created an iced strawberry layer cake decorated with bursting sparklers, which I served by the slice with tall, cool glasses of iced tea for the evening's main event.

Earlier in the day, however, cake combined with fresh fruit invariably takes center stage at the table. Our family's Independence Day celebrations are typically enjoyed either at the beach or the lake, as we find being near water helps quench the oppressive heat of summer. A light, fruit-filled trifle, presented in a trio of patriotic colors, adds not only to the decorative scheme, but also to the illusion of a cooling oasis at the height of summer's swell.

patriotic

When planning a celebration outdoors, I always try to include an "on the go" dessert—a touch that is particularly appreciated on an active holiday like the Fourth of July. Patriotic star-shaped sugar cookies, drizzled with tinted white chocolate, are presented in bouquet-like bunches on lollipop sticks so guests can grab and go as they enjoy their day. Not only do they tickle the sweet tooth, the cookies add an extra measure of eye appeal.

To me, one of the best things about summer in general, and Fourth of July in particular, is the abundance of fresh fruit that crops up about that time in farmers' markets, on trees, and in gardens across the South. Watermelon is a traditional favorite, but juicy strawberries, peaches, plums, and more are not only delicious eaten unadorned, but also the perfect antidote to summer's hottest days.

How do we slice a sheet cake? See Page 141

Overwhelmingly popular with the colonial settlers who introduced the traditional English dessert to America, the trifle remains a prized dish in the South. For this special Old Glory-inspired version, I painted split cake layers with a simple syrup, then layered the cubes of cake with blueberries, a mixture of strawberries and strawberry preserves, and whipped cream. The dessert's color lends itself to this particular holiday, and, as a bonus, the trifle also keeps well for long periods outdoors.

*N*ight Before Christmas

GROWING UP, THERE WAS NOTHING I LOOKED FORWARD TO QUITE AS MUCH as Christmas morning. The anticipation was so great, my sister Darri and I would even stage "rehearsals" before the big day, pretending to wake each other and race to the tree, twinkling with lights and standing cheerful sentry over the piles of presents just waiting to be unwrapped and enjoyed. By the time Christmas Eve arrived, the air seemed to crackle with excitement.

As an adult, I have found that holiday celebrations with my own children always seem to fall on the afternoon or evening of Christmas Day, causing the night before to lose a little of the luster I recall from my childhood. In an attempt to recapture the magic, my husband, Terry, and I host a special dinner each Christmas Eve for close friends and loved ones. The dining room table is placed next to the family-room hearth—where stockings ready to be filled hang, bordered by fresh magnolia leaves— allowing us to dine by the glow of the Christmas tree. For dessert, there is no choice more fitting than a towering gift-wrapped cake, which calls to mind the sweet anticipation of waiting for Christmas morning to arrive.

pink

So many people confine holiday decorating to traditional tones of red and green, but I like to branch out a little. The shade I chose for the gift-wrapped cakes served for this occasion is red enough to strike a holiday tone, yet pink enough to be unexpected. Covered with a thin layer of buttercream and then enrobed in fondant, each tier of the cake is made of a different flavor—red velvet, devil's food, and vanilla—and the entirety is lightly brushed with gold dust to resemble shiny foil wrapping. To keep the motif from becoming too overwhelming, the intricate scrollwork that adorns the top and bottom tiers is replaced with simple detailing on the middle layer. And although the dinner was intimate, I purposely made an extra large cake so each guest could take a portion home to enjoy on Christmas Day.

If any occasion merits the use of fine china and table linens, it is a Christmas Eve gathering. To accent the elegant place settings, I concentrated on gold accessories, which add plenty of seasonal sparkle while coordinating with the earth tones found in my home. Spiky, Art Deco-inspired gold Christmas trees form a unique centerpiece, especially when accented by a layer of shimmering fabric and a scattering of old-fashioned Christmas ornaments. When the dessert bell tolls, I like to transfer a few pillar candles from the foyer to the dining table to cast a warm glow on the cake as it is served.

christmas

Often, it is simply too warm in the South on Christmas to warrant a roaring fire—but I don't let that stop me from decorating our hearth. Bundles of fragrant pine mixed with fresh magnolia leaves, gathered from the tree in my mother's yard, serve as excellent holiday greenery. A weathered pail filled with pinecones and kindling plus oversized gold papier-mâché ornaments adds to the effect, and helps brighten up an otherwise dark hearth.

silver

Silver much like its sparkling cousin, gold, is a wonderful hue for holiday decorating. The silver dragees (decorative hard candies) on this package cake are stark but beautiful against the backdrop of white buttercream frosting. Resting on an ivory platter with a pierced holly-leaf pattern, the cake is placed over an ornament-filled trifle bowl that serves as a base for a sophisticated and unique cake stand.

children

When hosting a party I know will be attended by children, I always try to have a special table set up just for them. During the Christmas season at the bakery, we carry a wide selection of traditional holiday cakes that appeal to both children and adults. An assortment of these fanciful sweets makes a whimsical spread for the children's table, where they are presided over by one of my most cherished possessions—a vintage potbellied Santa that is actually a punchbowl. My parents purchased this treasure the year I was born and later handed it down to me.

How did we make these cakes sparkle? See Page 138

Here's how
we made and
did the things
you see.

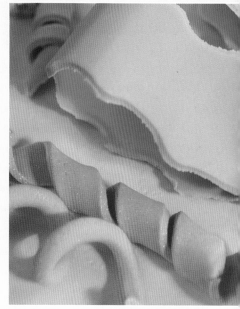

hints & how-tos

bows:

Package cakes resembling festive gift-wrapped presents are one of our most-requested items at Edgar's. The small square or round cakes can be decorated in any fashion, but their defining feature is the perfect, larger-than-life bow perched on top. These bows are deceptively simple to make—all you need to get started is a bit of fondant, a rolling pin, a butter knife or straight-edge spatula, and a one-inch dowel rod.

Step 1: Sprinkle a smooth surface with a bit of cornstarch. (Note: If creating a darker ribbon, such as brown, take care not to use too much cornstarch, as it will not blend as easily into darker colors.) Using a rolling pin, roll out the fondant in a thin layer (typically about ¼ inch thick). Using the heel of your hand, lightly smooth out any air bubbles.

Step 2: Using a ruler, measure sections of fondant to the desired width (the width of the ruler is generally a good guideline) and cut using a butter knife or straight-edge spatula. Drape short sections of fondant over a one-inch dowel rod and pinch at the ends. Once there are approximately 16 to 20 ribbon sections, let them dry at least six to eight hours on the dowel rod.

Step 3: To assemble bow, place a mound of fondant or buttercream frosting in the center of the cake. Insert ribbon pieces into the mound, turning every other one, until bow is complete.

hint:

Kneading fondant serves several purposes. First, it can allow you to integrate color—typically, a drop or two of food coloring in the center of a ball of fondant is all that's needed to saturate it with color. In addition, kneading can also be useful if the fondant is beginning to dry as you're still working with it. The natural oils in your hands will help to revive it temporarily so you can continue working. However, it's very important to note that kneading fondant is not like kneading bread or pie crust dough—rather than folding it over on itself, you simply want to pound it down on the countertop. Folding will create air bubbles—the scourge of any cake decorator trying to achieve a smooth surface.

ribbons:

The same technique used to make the large bows for package cakes can also be used to make a variety of different styles of fondant ribbons for different types of cakes. For the party hat birthday cakes in Hat Trick, page 50, I used thick, wavy streamers to personalize the cakes and thin curlicues to top the party hats.

To make streamers, cut fairly wide strips of fondant and trim the ends at an angle, as you would for making a package bow. Rather than pinching the ends together, lay the strip lightly across a crumpled paper towel. As it dries, the fondant will hold the waves that are created by the wrinkles in the towel, adding unique texture.

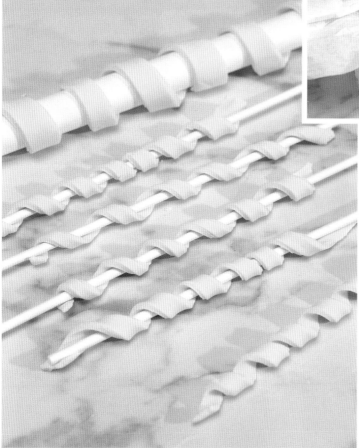

For curlicue ribbons, roll out the fondant and cut into thin strips, about ¼ or ½ inch wide. Wind the strips in a spiral around a lollipop stick or small dowel rod, and let them dry. Within about five minutes, the fondant should hold its shape enough to allow you to slide the curlicue off the stick; however, make sure the fondant is completely dry (let it rest six to eight hours) before attaching the curlicues to your cake.

flowers:

Although hand-crafted gum-paste flowers, such as the sunflowers shown in April Showers, page 70, can often be time-consuming to construct, creating basic flowers from rolled fondant is quite simple. Gum-paste cutters are available in all sorts of shapes and sizes, allowing you to press a wide variety of blooms from the fondant. Once you've added the desired details to your flowers, they can be left to dry or attached immediately to the cake with a dab of corn syrup or buttercream frosting.

tips:

A good selection of stainless-steel decorating tips is a must for any cake decorator. Depending on the tip you attach to the end of your buttercream-filled pastry bag, you can fashion a variety of different flowers and leaves. Each tip produces a design so specific that you can fine-tune the types of leaves (a calla lily leaf versus a rose leaf) and flowers (a wild rose versus a tea rose), based on which tip is used. Although floral decorations are the primary application for which I use tips, with a little creativity, certain tips can also be adapted for other uses. To make the feathers on our popular hen cake, featured in Farm Fresh, page 36, I used a tip that is normally employed to create leaf embellishments.

hat brim:

Created from rolled fondant, the wavy brim of our Kentucky Derby hat was cut from a slab of fondant and formed over rolled plastic wrap. As the fondant dried, the brim held the natural waves imparted by the plastic wrap.

hint:

One of my favorite tricks for making my creations just a little bit more special is using edible glitter or pearl dust. This sparkly powder is available in any color imaginable, and it can be brushed on lightly for a subtle shimmer, or mixed with any clear alcohol, such as vodka (adding water will cause the powder to break down), and painted on for a more saturated sheen.

slicing cake:

Cutting cake, especially for large groups and parties, is no easy feat. These slicing tips will give pretty even pieces every time.

Sheet Cake: When cutting a sheet cake, it's best to cut the length of one side completely and then divide into even portions. This method keeps the slices a consistent depth for the entire length of the cake. Eye the width of each slice on the first row, then cut the remaining cake following the same steps. When cutting a sheet cake, you don't have to worry about slices falling over or crumbling, so focus instead on the consistency of the slices, and then plate an entire row of cake at one time. To do so, place the cake server under each slice, using the cutting knife to slide the cake off the server and onto the plate.

Round Cake: First, determine how many servings you will need. Thin slices yield more servings and tend to have a better appearance on the plate than wedges. To cut, start by slicing the cake down the center. After one half is cut into two quarters, measure with your eye to determine how thick you want each serving. Begin slicing on one end. Because layer cake slices tend to topple over, place your hand or cake server next to the slice you are cutting and allow the slice to rest on the server. Balancing the cake on the server with the knife, guide the slice onto the plate, using the knife to slide the cake off the server onto the plate. The first piece of sliced cake tends to have an abundance of icing. Reserve this piece for the sugar lover in your house.

hint:

The trick to cutting cake into picture-perfect slices is keeping the knife clean. Keep a damp tea towel on the back of the serving table and, after cutting each slice, place the knife inside the fold of the towel and slide the knife through. Also, I prefer to use a long, serrated knife when cutting cake.

ordering a cake:

Over the years, I have seen people make every mistake possible when it comes to ordering a cake. Most often, their faux pas fall into one of two categories: either, due to a lack of time or imagination, they are forced to order a generic, uninspiring sheet cake for their event, or else they arrive at the bakery with a picture of an elaborate creation they've come across and then are shocked to hear what such a confection costs. At Edgar's, we try to minimize these extremes by offering cakes that are gorgeous and unique—but that won't cause you to have to dip into your savings account. When you order exclusively designed cakes like the ones our talented, artistic decorators create, there are a few things to keep in mind.

Find a baker you can trust. For a good baker, creating cakes is a work of art and, therefore, the ability to employ artistic freedom within a set of guidelines is essential. Only a trusting relationship will produce an end result that is pleasing to both parties. Along the same lines, I highly recommend choosing a professional bakery to create cakes for special events. Many bakers who operate from their homes, while undoubtedly talented, do not have the resources to handle unexpected emergencies. If you decide to go this route, again, make sure you've found a person you can trust to come through with the cake for your event.

Know with whom you should speak with at the bakery. Many people will want to speak directly to the decorator, but at most large bakeries, this isn't feasible. At Edgar's, we have a highly trained team of customer service representatives who facilitate all cake orders. Above all, make sure the person taking your order is both knowledgeable and courteous. If not, you have every right to voice your concern to a manager. After all, you would not want your special day jeopardized by an inexperienced staff member. Unusual questions that have the service staff stumped can always be taken to the decorator. And for weddings, seek out the staff wedding coordinator to ensure you receive personalized service for such an important day.

Refrain from ordering your cake on the busiest days of the year. You'll almost certainly get better customer service if you wait a day or two. As a rule, the day before a major holiday will be chaotic, but try to avoid these in particular: Christmas Eve, the Saturday before Easter, the Wednesday before Thanksgiving, and the Saturdays before Mother's Day and Father's Day.

Do your homework before you go. Arrive at your bakery with answers prepared for following questions, and the entire process will go much more smoothly.

- How many people do you plan to serve?
- When is the party? Guests will generally eat more cake at an afternoon tea, for example, than after a large dinner.
- Who will be attending? This information is essential in determining the number of servings you will need. In general, it holds true that women eat less than men. This is a good rule of thumb, but if you happen to know the eating habits of your guests, it will make your estimate that much more accurate.
- Where will the cake be displayed? The amount of space you have to display the cake may affect its shape and size.
- What is a serving size? Edgar's uses a common slicing system that is typical of many bakeries, but each bakery is different. The same cake could serve from 12 to 20 people, depending on how it is sliced.

when to order:

At Edgar's, we have a very tight decorating schedule that is almost akin to the appointments calendar at a doctor's office. People often feel that if they order a cake at the last minute, it will be fresher, but that is never the case at our bakery—our layers are baked to order and are never frozen. I recommend ordering at least a week in advance to ensure that a decorator will be available to craft your cake. At the very least, order no later than 48 hours in advance, as this is the minimum amount of time it takes for this creation. The steps detailed below should give you an idea of the process your cake will go through, from conception to completion.

Two days before the event: Cake is baked and cooled to room temperature, wrapped in plastic wrap to keep air out, and placed in the walk-in cooler.

One day before the event: At around mid-day, the cake is removed from the cooler and iced, then detailed by the decorator. Once finished, the cake is boxed.

Day of the event: The boxed cake is usually ready for the customer to pick up by the morning of the party. For Saturday events, decorators often have to work into the wee hours of the morning to have the cakes completed and ready for pick-up.

picking up a cake:

Believe it or not, there is a right time and a wrong time to pick up a cake for an event. The following dos and don'ts should help you avoid frustration and last-minute catastrophes:

Don't pick up your cake on the way to the party—this is a recipe for disaster. We've repaired many a cake that was the victim of a sudden stop or a misstep on the way to an event.

Do arrange for someone to pick up the cake at least several hours in advance, or preferably the day before the party. If the layers are baked fresh, most cakes will still taste delicious the next day—and that's one less task you have to worry about the day of your event.

Don't try to pick up the cake before your scheduled time—doing so will almost always guarantee frustration. On busy days, decorators are often scheduled to finish the cake the hour the customer will pick it up, so chances are if you arrive early, your cake won't be ready.

Do check the cake before you leave the bakery. If someone else is picking up the cake on your behalf, make sure they know how it should look. You don't want to wait until the party to discover that a name has been misspelled or the cake has been iced in the wrong flavor.

Don't be afraid to speak up if something is wrong with your cake. Most flaws are minor and can be corrected in a matter of minutes or hours. I would never want any of my customers to walk away unhappy with their cakes, nor would most other bakers.

Do transport the cake on a level surface. The front seat of your car is probably the worst place to set a cake—one sudden stop, and you have a disaster on your hands. The back of an SUV is the ideal place to transport a cake, but any flat surface will work. Still, be sure to drive slowly and carefully!

Don't try to transport a cake in the trunk of your car. The flat surface is desirable, yes, but heat and exhaust fumes are more likely to seep in and ruin the cake.

embellishments: fruits & flowers

Not everyone is born with the ability to paint great masterpieces, write beautiful sonatas or pen lovely poems, nor does everyone come equipped with the dexterity and skill required to decorate showstopping cakes. I count it as one of my greatest blessings that God granted me the gift of creating artful cakes. Sometimes, however, the prettiest adornments for cakes are not to be found in a pastry tube or a sheet of fondant, but rather in your favorite fruit bowl or flower garden. And the nicest part, aside from the relative ease with which you can embellish your own beautiful cakes, is that while an experienced hand with delicate decorations is not required, the use of your creativity is.

embellishments: sugar on top

If Picasso had his paints, I have my sugar. Though I have been in the cake-baking business for some time now, it never fails to amaze me how versatile sugar actually is. From just a few cups, you can create an endless number of confections, cakes, and embellishments. Sugared fruit is one of my favorite ways to use the sweet stuff as a decorative tool. The naturally beautiful shapes and colors of the fruit glisten even more with a sparkling coat of sugar. Another, even simpler, way to add decorative and taste appeal is through the use of glazes. Made with confectioner's sugar and cream, water, or fruit nectar, a drizzle of glaze adds a sweet and tasteful finishing touch to cakes. If you wish to keep the color creamy white but want to add a dash of flavor, try your hand with a drop or two of extract, available in a variety of flavors and located on the spices aisle of most grocery stores.

hint:

To sugar your own fruit, first wash each piece in cool water, pat dry, then evenly coat with either meringue powder mixed with water or—if the fruit will not be eaten—egg whites. Hold fruit in one hand, and with the other, evenly sprinkle sugar on all sides. Place on a rack to dry and harden. For best results, use super-fine sugar.

cake basics:

Baking and icing a cake can be one of the most rewarding things you will do in your home kitchen. The act of crafting a cake can be gift to your family, a way to honor your friends, and a way to satisfy your creative spirit. The following recipes are tried and true basic cakes and icings from which you can create an infinite number of cake expressions.

carrot cake

Long before Terry and I opened Edgar's, my sister Nancy's carrot cake was a family favorite. We counted on her recipe to be the special dessert at the end of every holiday meal.

1 ½ cups vegetable oil
2 cups sugar
4 extra-large eggs
2 cups grated fresh carrots
1 (8-ounce) can crushed pineapple in juice
2 ¼ cups all-purpose flour
1 teaspoon baking powder
½ teaspoon baking soda
½ teaspoon nutmeg
2 teaspoons cinnamon
1 teaspoon salt
½ cup raisins
½ cup chopped pecans

Preheat oven to 360°. Grease two 8-inch round cake pans and dust with flour. Mix together vegetable oil, sugar, eggs, carrots, pineapple, flour, baking powder, baking soda, nutmeg, cinnamon, and salt until well-blended. Stir in raisins and pecans; pour batter into prepared pans. Bake 35-45 minutes, or until golden brown. Layers should spring back to the touch when removed from oven. Cool in pans before turning onto cooling racks.

hint: For the best results, wrap cooled layers tightly in plastic wrap to keep any moisture from escaping, and place them upside down in the refrigerator overnight. This will make the layers much easier to ice the next day.

cream cheese frosting

Pair this creamy icing with our Carrot Cake, and your guests will be back for seconds.

¼ cup unsalted butter or margarine
1 (8-ounce) package cream cheese
4 cups confectioners' sugar
1 tablespoon vanilla

In large bowl and using electric mixer at high speed, combine butter, cream cheese, confectioners' sugar, and vanilla; cream until smooth.

hint: Allow butter or margarine and cream cheese to come to room temperature before mixing, which will make creaming and spreading will be much easier.

white cake

Special occasions just seem to call for elegant cakes with pristine white layers. This basic cake works well with buttercream icing.

2 ¼ cup sifted cake flour
1 ½ cup sugar
3 ½ teaspoons baking powder
1 teaspoon salt
½ cup shortening
1 cup milk
1 ½ teaspoons vanilla extract
4 egg whites, unbeaten

Preheat oven to 350°. Lightly grease and flour two 9-inch cake pans. In large bowl, sift together cake flour, sugar, baking powder, and salt. Add shortening, and using electric mixer at low speed, beat in ¾ cup milk and vanilla extract until just combined. At medium speed, beat prepared mixture two minutes, occasionally scraping down sides of bowl; add remaining milk, then beat in egg whites. Divide batter between prepared pans; bake 26-28 minutes, or until cake tester inserted in center comes out clean. Cool in pans on wire rack 10 minutes. Remove from pans and cool completely.

yellow cake

A yellow cake, dense and moist, is essential to every baker's repertoire. The recipe will serve a variety of purposes when paired with a flavorful icing.

3 cups sifted cake flour
2 ½ teaspoons baking powder
1 teaspoon salt
¾ cup butter, softened
1 ½ cups sugar
3 eggs
2 teaspoons vanilla
1 cup milk

Preheat oven to 350°. Lightly grease and flour two 9-inch cake pans. In medium bowl, sift cake flour with baking powder. In large bowl and using electric mixer at high speed, beat butter, sugar, eggs, and vanilla until light and fluffy (about 6 minutes), occasionally scraping down sides of bowl. At low speed, beat in cake flour mixture, alternating with milk (beginning and ending with flour mixture) until just smooth. Divide batter between prepared pans, and bake 28-30 minutes or until cake tester inserted in center comes out clean. Cool in pans on wire rack 10 minutes. Remove from pans and cool completely.

chocolate cake

This recipe makes a chocolate cake that is saturated with the rich flavor of cocoa.

2 ¼ cups all-purpose flour
2 cups sugar
¾ cups unsweetened natural cocoa powder
1 ½ teaspoons baking soda
1 teaspoon baking powder
½ teaspoon salt
1 cup vegetable oil
1 cup strong coffee
3 eggs
1 (8-ounce) container sour cream
1 teaspoon vanilla extract

Preheat oven to 325°. Grease and flour three 8-inch cake pans. In large bowl, combine flour, sugar, cocoa powder, baking soda, baking powder, and salt. Add oil, coffee, and eggs, and using electric mixer at medium speed, beat 2 minutes, or until combined. Stir in sour cream and vanilla. Divide batter between prepared pans. Bake 28-30 minutes, or until cake tester inserted in center comes out clean. Cool in pans on wire rack 10 minutes. Remove from pans and cool completely on wire rack.

chocolate buttercream icing

My dad's favorite cake is my mom's yellow cake with chocolate frosting. This recipe for icing is very simple, but the best things in life always are, aren't they?

4 cups confectioners' sugar
$\frac{1}{2}$ cup unsalted butter or margarine, melted
4 teaspoons cocoa powder
Water for consistency

In large bowl, combine cocoa and sugar until well-blended, with no lumps. Add melted butter and using electric mixer at medium speed, blend well. Add water, 1 teaspoon at a time, and blend until mixture reaches spreading consistency.

petit four icing

Petit four icing is very popular, and our sugar-sweet version is easy to make.

$\frac{1}{2}$ cup vegetable oil
$\frac{1}{2}$ cup whole milk
6 $\frac{1}{2}$ cups confectioners' sugar
1 teaspoon vanilla extract

Combine oil and milk in microwave-safe container. Warm mixture in microwave approximately 5 minutes on high power, then 1 minute on regular power, stirring between. Pour into large bowl. Using electric mixer fitted with paddle, beat on low speed, adding $\frac{1}{4}$ cup sugar at a time. Mix until consistency is sticky to touch, but pours easily. Mix in vanilla extract. Use immediately or refrigerate. Icing will keep up to three days, refrigerated. To reheat, add small amount warm milk and stir until pouring consistency.

hint: When making petit four icing, use caution to avoid overheating. Be patient and stir often.

royal icing

This icing is great for topping cookies you plan to decorate. It hardens as it dries, making it a perfect choice for ease of handling.

$\frac{1}{4}$ cup meringue powder
1 teaspoon vanilla extract
$\frac{1}{2}$ cup water
7 cups confectioners' sugar

In large bowl and using electric mixer at slow speed, combine meringue powder and water. Mix 1 minute. Increase speed to high and beat 3-5 minutes until soft peaks form. Add sugar and vanilla. Mix on medium speed until smooth.

hint: For thinner icing that can be poured, add slightly more water until mixture reaches desired consistency. This icing will keep up to three days at room temperature.

Resources

*Items not listed are either antiques
or from a private collection*

Serene Setting • Pages 16-21
White pitchers (used as vases): Harmony Landing

Run For the Roses • Pages 22-29
Cake stands: Edgar's Bakery
Crystal flower vase and bowl: Table Matters
Red placemats: Lamb's Ears Ltd.
Cake server: Table Matters
Plates: Christine's
Napkins: Edgar's Bakery

Adventures in Cake • Pages 30-35
Tea service, tablecloths, and napkins: Christine's

Farm Fresh • Pages 36-43
Three-tiered server: Summerhill Ltd.
Children's dinnerware and centerpieces: Christine's

Pumpkin Patch • Pages 44-47
Dishes, chargers, vase, and mugs: Harmony Landing
Cake stand: Summerhill Ltd.

Hat Trick • Pages 50-57
White candleholders (used as cake stands),
    glass plates: At Home Furnishings
Votive bowls, vases, napkins on plate: Harmony Landing
Cocktail napkins: Table Matters
Parfait glasses: Summerhill Ltd.
Party hats: Edgar's Bakery
Ruffled ribbons: Elaine's

Sweet Surprise • Pages 58-61
Napkins: Table Matters
Crystal cake stands: Edgar's Bakery
Plates, napkins, cake server: Christine's
Plates: Target
Tablecloth: Martha Lauren's Antique Linens & Accessories

Bridal Charm • Pages 62-69
Cake topper: Edgar's Bakery

April Showers • Pages 70-77
Cake stands: Edgar's Bakery
Cake servers: Christine's
Floral arrangement: Dorothy McDaniel's Flower Market

Directory

At Home Furnishings
2921 18th Street South
Homewood, AL 35209
205-879-3510

Beverly Ruff Antiques and Linens
3232 Cahaba Heights Road
Vestavia Hills, AL 35243
205-262-9434

Blooms
2518 18th Street South
Homewood, AL 35209
205-969-0705

Christine's
2822 Petticoat Lane
Mountain Brook, AL 35223
205-871-8297

Dorothy McDaniel's Flower Market
2560 18th Street South
Homewood, AL 35209
205-871-0092

Edgar's Bakery
499 Southgate Drive
Pelham, AL 35124
205-987-0790

Edgewood Fine Jewelry
934 Oxmoor Road
Homewood, AL 35209
205-423-8616

Elaine's
860 Plantation Way
Montgomery, AL 36117
800-811-3742

Harmony Landing
2925 18th Street South
Homewood, AL 35209
205-871-0585

HomeGoods
1656 Montgomery Highway
Birmingham, AL 35226
205-823-5221

Homewood Florist
940 Oxmoor Road
Homewood, AL 35209
205-870-8809

Interiors at Pepper Place
2817 Second Avenue South
Birmingham, AL 35233
205-323-2817

Lamb's Ears Ltd.
3138 Cahaba Heights Road
Vestavia Hills, AL 35243
205-969-3138

Martha Lauren's Antique Linens
& Accessories
2417 Canterbury Road
Mountain Brook, AL 35223
205-871-2283

Summerhill Ltd.
2901 18th Street South
Homewood, AL 35209
205-871-2902

Table Matters
2402 Montevallo Road
Mountain Brook, AL 35223
205-879-0125

Target
4616 Highway 280
Birmingham, AL 35242
205-408-7687